LEGENDS of CORNWALL

Sally Jones

BOSSINEY BOOKS

First published in 1980
by Bossiney Books
St Teath, Bodmin, Cornwall
Designed, typeset and printed in Great Britain by
Penwell Ltd, Parkwood, Callington,
Cornwall

© Sally Jones 1980

ISBN O 906456 36 3

PLATE ACKNOWLEDGEMENTS

Cover photograph by Murray King
Drawings by Paul Honeywill
Pages 55, 80, 84, 86, back cover John Chard
Pages 11, 36, 37, 41, 45, 46 Alice Lennox-Boyd
Pages 5, 7, 33, 34, 69, 71, 76, 77, 82, 91, 93, 96 Murray King
Pages 57, 60, 61 by courtesy of
the Royal Institution of Cornwall
Pages 54, 98 David Clarke
Pages 75, 79 David Mudd
Page 68 John Wanstall
All other photographs by Ray Bishop

*Author and Publisher are indebted to Mr and Mrs Peter Richards of the Rosehill
Riding School, Penzance, for lending their horse, Bodrifty, to be photographed at
Men-an-Tol for the cover of this book.*

ABOUT THE AUTHOR

Not for nothing has Cornwall been called the Land of Legend. Myth, down the ages, has triggered all the great storytelling. Here Sally Jones introduces us to some beautiful parts of this magical landscape and brings to life some of the great Cornish tales so vividly that we begin to wonder if there can be any smoke without fire. Of her journey that began at Tamar, telling how the great river came into being and got its name, and ended at Land's End where Lyonesse seems very close to the surface, she hopes others will 'follow in my footsteps and experience that splendid thrill of discovery . . .'

This then is more than a collection of stories. It's a book of exploration, encouraging us to see the changing countryside and the coast that does daily battle with the sea. Words, reinforced by beautiful drawings of legendary characters and fine photographs of the legendary sites, all combine to bring us back in time — and feel that timeless quality that makes Cornwall a people and a place apart.

Sally Jones was educated at King Edward VI High School for Girls, Birmingham, and read English at St Hugh's College, Oxford, where she won five Blues — tennis, squash, modern pentathlon, netball and cricket. She was British Schoolgirl tennis champion and has played squash for Devon and tennis and squash for Warwickshire. In 1976 she won the *Sunday Telegraph* writing prize of £500 for an account of a tour of Ireland with the British Universities tennis team. More recently she won a prize in the Catherine Pakenham Memorial Awards for Young Women Journalists. In 1978 she joined the BBC as a News Trainee and the following year she moved to Westward TV as a television reporter on Westward Diary.

LEGENDS of CORNWALL

What is legend but gossip grown old?

Certainly the legends of Cornwall make a fascinating patchwork of gossip, scandal and anecdote. Some deal with real people, historical figures whose life stories have been embellished with a generous helping of exaggeration and the supernatural. Cornwall's most notorious villain, Tregeagle, the wicked steward of Lanhydrock definitely existed in the seventeenth century, though if he'd actually accomplished all the frightful things he's credited with — marrying heiresses and murdering them for their money, just for starters — he'd have had little time for his more orthodox activities like running the estate. Other characters are more dubious. Giants stride through many legends, eating children, burying treasure or hurling the massive stone quoits which now dominate so many moorland hilltops. One coffin dug up at Tregony in the seventeenth century measured 11 feet and contained a tooth 2½ inches long. Elsewhere the skeletons of abnormally tall men have been unearthed, though as yet none large enough to have stood with one foot in Carn Brea and the other in St Agnes, six miles away as the crow flies, a feat attributed to the picturesquely named Giant Bolster.

Prosaic archaeologists declare the quoits to be Stone-Age tombs, erected up to 4,000 years ago by megalith builders for the families of their priestly chiefs. Some try to explain the legends of the giants themselves as the natural reaction of the Cornish to the series of invasions by taller, more economically dominant races: Anglo-Saxons, Danes and Normans. Similarly, the groups of standing stones found throughout Cornwall are now thought to be the temples and amphitheatres of Prehistoric men and historians sniffily dismiss the enchanting idea that they are girls turned to

**Enys Dodman and Armed Knight, Land's End:
'Not for nothing has Cornwall been called the Land of Legend.'▶**

stone for dancing on the Sabbath as the pious attempt by Medieval Christianity to lend a moral to these stark monuments.

Whatever the source of the tales though, nothing can spoil their narrative vigour or weaken the peculiar power they share with all the greatest myths, folk tales and fairy stories. This power perhaps stems from their combination of earthy realism and seductive fantasy. It is a combination which in one legend can produce touches of wry, down-to-earth humour typical of the Cornish, while in another it can create a truly terrifying ghost story, all the more compelling because it is rooted so firmly in reality.

Thousands of legends survive, many recorded by scholars and antiquarians after being passed down orally in a variety of versions by generations of fireside gossips. In a book of this scope, the great problem is selection as the compiler is literally spoilt for choice. My method has been a purely self-indulgent one, collecting as many legends and their different versions as I could find and choosing only those which particularly caught my imagination, using the familiar prickle at the top of the spine as the touchstone of a good ghost story.

The legends are taken from all over Cornwall and arranged geographically in the form of a journey for the benefit of people who enjoy seeking out their nearby sites. I found this a marvellous way to explore the timeless landscapes of Cornwall where the memorials of Stone-Age men, the Medieval monasteries and cells, the stark ruins of the nineteenth century are all constant reminders of a past more strange, hard, and dangerous than our own. It's a past which lives on in the legends and in the minds of Cornish men and women where it is as vivid and real as the present day.

THE ORIGIN OF THE RIVER TAMAR

The broad silver flood of the River Tamar forms a magically beautiful boundary between Devon and Cornwall. It rises near Bude, so close to the north coast that Cornwall is all but an island and correspondingly conscious of its uniqueness and isolation. The river has an equally lovely legend associated with its origin, as

Dr Johnson's Head: 'the great cliffs at Land's End.'▶

grand and strange as any classical myth of transformation.

A beautiful nymph, Tamara, was born in a cavern, the daughter of two spirits of the earth. In contrast to her dull strict parents, she loved the upper world, revelling in the warmth of the sun and the birdsong that they shunned. She escaped from the cavern whenever she could to swim in the streams and bound over the hills of Dartmoor. Here it was that she captured the hearts of two young giants, Tavy and Tawrage, who lived on the moor and followed wherever she led them. Each loved her to distraction and pleaded with her to choose between them to put them out of their misery. Tamara loved the excitement of their admiration, like any young girl learning to flirt and allure, and at first pretended not to take them seriously, leading them a merry dance over the moors like a will-o'-the-wisp. She would linger until they were nearly on her then waltz away, teasing and tantalizing.

At last, under a bush in Morwenstow, she consented to listen to their pleading, but by now her testy father had arrived to force her back to the cavern, a scene which has been enacted at countless discos but never with such far-reaching results. She refused to leave her lovers and in fury, her father screeched out a spell which cast Tavy and Tawrage into a deep sleep. Then he turned her into a limpid stream, bubbling from a marshy meadow, at first trickling slowly through the boggy ground, then burbling into deep brown pools at the heart of the woods and finally flowing majestically into the sea, as the great River Tamar.

The giants awoke and rushed home in despair. Tavy dashed into his father's hall, close to suicide, and his father, realising that his son could not survive without his beloved, transformed the youth into the stream which now bears his name. He meandered hither and thither, calling to his love, until their two streams mingled and flowed together into the sea.

In the depths of despair, Tawrage sought out an enchanter and was changed likewise into a river, now called the Taw, but sadly for him he lost his way and flowed in the opposite direction from his adored Tamara. They say he still mourns as he glides, searching fruitlessly for her for ever.

The origin of the Tamar: 'Her father
screeched out a spell which cast Tavy and Tawrage into a deep sleep.'▶

▲'The broad silver flood of the River Tamar . . a magically beautiful boundary.'

The Tamar at Calstock viaduct▼

THE WITCH OF ANTONY

A few miles into Cornwall is the village of Antony, scene of a strange tale of malice and enchantment. In the story the traditional roles of heartless landlord and pathetic tenant are reversed — literally — with a vengeance.

An old woman known as Aunt Alsey, who lived in Antony had earned herself the title of witch, more through her violent moods and rages than by her supernatural skills. She lived in a tiny terraced house owned by a kindly shopkeeper in Devonport and, after she had refused to pay any rent for several years, he crossed the Tamar Bridge, plucking up courage to turn the old harridan out of her cottage.

She was more than a match for him and seating herself firmly in the doorway she called down a terrible curse on the man, his wife and the child she was carrying. Horrified at the concentrated spite in the old woman's cracked voice, the man rushed away in terror and returning home told his wife and daughter all that had happened. They listened, then went back to the counter to weigh out some

The village of Antony

goods for their customers, chatting gaily as they always did. Suddenly a thump and a heavy crash interrupted the talk. A huge toad had dropped onto the scales from the ceiling of the shop and sprawled there, puffing itself up furiously. The man hastily snatched up a pair of tongs and grasping the swollen creature flung it into the fire, almost retching at its ugliness.

His wife, meanwhile, had fainted and suffered a series of fits each time she came to. When the doctor was called he told her husband to prepare for a premature birth and the two men busied themselves with making the moaning woman comfortable.

From the living room the couple's daughter let out a terrible shriek.

'Father! The toad! The toad!' The man rushed downstairs and found that the toad had escaped death and though dreadfully burned had crawled painfully over the blazing logs and now sat spitting in the fender. As they gazed in horror, a man arrived from Antony to fetch both doctor and shopkeeper, saying that Aunt Alsey had fallen into the fire in a fit, setting the rest of the house alight and nearly burning herself to death. Shuddering, the shopkeeper threw the toad out onto one of the flowerbeds before hurrying to Antony to find the house gutted and the old woman mortally stricken. She died within a few minutes and when he went home the man found the toad dead, with exactly the same burns as the old woman had sustained.

The witch's curse evidently worked beyond the grave for the wife almost died in childbirth and the son she bore grew up handsome and charming but was lost at sea whilst he was still a young man.

CRUEL COPPINGER

Following Cornwall's boundary to the north coast, I was told the famous legend of Cruel Coppinger by an elderly lady living near Bude. She also sang the verse which follows, set to a familiar folk tune, and the inexplicable menace of the tale caught my imagination at once.

Few Cornish villains are more strange and mysterious than the

◄The Witch of Antony: 'She called down a terrible curse.'

Dane known as Cruel Coppinger, although he is no mere legend, having definitely lived at the end of the eighteenth century. North Cornwall was a relatively peaceful place by then, the series of foreign invaders long since gone and even the notorious smugglers and wreckers far more evident in fiction than in fact. All this was to change when one black, stormy night a foreign ship was wrecked off Welcombe Mouth on the treacherous north coast of Cornwall.

In full view of the helpless watchers on the shore, everyone aboard was drowned in the towering waves or battered to death on the rocks, except for one man, a huge broad figure who clawed his way through the seething surf and reached the beach against all odds. Spitting and brushing his mane of hair from his eyes, he snatched a cloak from an old woman standing nearby. Then, despite his exhaustion, he vaulted up behind a young girl on a horse which he spurred off into the night. They galloped home to the farm where the girl, Dinah Hamlyn, lived with her parents. Here the stranger was welcomed like one of the family, given food and dry clothes and eventually a job as farm labourer.

The Hamlyns discovered that he was a Dane named David Coppinger, although he never mentioned his past, but worked doggedly with the strength of five men. The workers in their turn found that he had a violent temper which he contrived to hide from the Hamlyns, preferring instead to pay court to the unsophisticated Dinah whose head was turned by the attentions of the tall, unpredictable stranger.

A few months later, Farmer Hamlyn died and after an indecently short interval Coppinger married Dinah, taking over the farm. Soon his true character began to surface and he showed himself a brutal and sadistic husband and employer. Even the son Dinah bore him was a deaf-and-dumb idiot and possessed his father's callousness to such a degree that the local people all swore he had been born without a soul. Coppinger let the farm go to rack and ruin and turned back to the sea for his livelihood, not as a sailor or fisherman but as the savage leader of a gang of wreckers and smugglers. They showed no mercy to shipwrecked sailors or excisemen who had the misfortune to catch them at their evil work. Even those reluctant to join the gang were persuasively pressed into the Dane's service,

Cruel Coppinger: '... savage leader of a gang of wreckers.' ▶

usually with the butt end of a pistol. Eventually the forces of the law and revenue banded together and made the County too hot to hold the terrifying villain, so one night during a howling storm like the one that had brought him to Cornwall, Coppinger boarded a strange vessel and sailed away. His memory lives on in numerous drolls, colourful tales and verses like:

Will you hear of Cruel Coppinger,
He came from a foreign land,
He was brought to us by salt water,
He was carried away by the wind.

THE BELLS OF FORRABURY CHURCH

Further down the coast, at Boscastle, the Forrabury Church provides a great contrast to its neighbour at Tintagel, for although the latter's bells ring out each Sunday, the tower of Forrabury has stood silent for centuries. Long ago the people of Forrabury decided on a peal of bells to rival those of Tintagel. After they had been cast and blessed, the bells were shipped to Forrabury, and as the voyage was calm, the boat was soon standing off Tintagel head, waiting for the tide to carry her into Boscastle Harbour.

The pilot heard the vesper bells at Tintagel and kneeling down he crossed himself and thanked God for their speedy voyage. At this the captain laughed loudly, saying that the pilot was a superstitious fool and swearing that his skill alone had ensured the ship's safety. The pilot protested at this profanity, but the captain laughed louder than ever and declared that all they now needed was the pilot's judgement for a happy landing.

'May God forgive you,' said the pilot. He evidently hoped in vain for a great wave rose up, far out to sea, and rolled on inexorably, destroying everything in its path. It overwhelmed the ship which sank instantly less than half a mile from land with loss of all hands except the God-fearing pilot. As the ship went down, the new bells tolled with a muffled sound as if they were ringing her death-knell. To this day the church tower has remained mute, but the people of Forrabury swear that when storms are coming, the bells ring dully from beneath the waves to warn of the approaching bad weather and remind the godless of God's retribution.

16

The Author at Forrabury churchyard

KING ARTHUR IN NORTH CORNWALL

The very mention of Tintagel invokes the name King Arthur, for although many parts of Britain — and Brittany — claim him as their own, the work of writers from Geoffrey of Monmouth in the twelfth century to Alfred, Lord Tennyson has set him as folk hero and symbol of peerless nobility squarely in Cornwall. The historical Arthur is a shadowy figure who first appears in the *Historia Britonum*, a compilation completed around 685. He defeated the Saxons in twelve battles, the tenth at Chester and the last at Mons Badonis, the Badon Hill victory of about 500, when we learn that '960 men fell before the assault of Arthur and no one felled them save he alone'. This was the brief and matter-of-fact birth of a myth which captured the imagination of Western Europe, flowering most luxuriantly when the old ideals of courage and self-sacrifice which Arthur represented seemed most threatened.

▲Tintagel Headland: '… jutting out into the Atlantic like a great ship.'

Tintagel Castle ruins▶

The reality of Arthur the obscure chieftain, though fascinating to detective-historians, is infinitely less potent and compelling than the legends which haunt every corner of Cornwall. It would be almost impossible to visit each site connected with Arthur, but a tour of the best-known provides a spectacular diversity of landscape and a wealth of classic tales of magic and adventure.

Tintagel Castle has become a place of pilgrimage as Arthur's legendary birthplace and home and despite the inevitable commercialisation of the town itself which even boasts 'King Arthur's car park' and 'gift shoppe', the castle, the ruinous skeleton of a Norman fortress, keeps its austere power, aloof from crass exploitation and gushing trippers. These ruins now seem an almost organic part of the rugged headland, jutting out into the Atlantic like a great ship putting out to sea. Erosion by centuries of waves has nibbled away the isthmus connecting it to the mainland, which even in Geoffrey of Monmouth's day was 'so narrow that three

18

◄The Author at Tintagel Castle ...

         ... 'the ruinous skeleton of a Norman fortress.'▲

armed knights might hold it against the entire realm of Britain'.
The stronghold is now all but an island, more romantic than ever
with its narrow path of stone-hewn steps and sheer towering cliffs of
black slate.

It is easy to imagine why Gorlois, Duke of Cornwall, kept his
beautiful wife, Ygraine, locked in Tintagel in a vain attempt to
prevent the infatuated British king, Uther Pendragon, from seeing
her. Merlin the magician concocted a magic potion which
transformed Uther into the double of Gorlois. Thus disguised, he
walked openly into the castle and slept with Ygraine, a neat
supernatural solution which enhanced Merlin's skill and Uther's
reputation for cunning while preserving Ygraine's wifely virtue.
Arthur was the result of the union and soon afterwards his parents
were joined in legal wedlock, for Uther defeated and slew Gorlois in
battle at St Dennis, then took Ygraine as his wife and Queen.

Merlin, whose cave lies at the base of the headland directly below

21

the castle is said to have taken the infant Arthur and fostered him with Sir Ector and his family, ensuring the child's safety by keeping his parentage a closely-guarded secret. It seems strange that such a powerful magician as Merlin should choose to live in such discomfort, for his cave is invaded by the sea at high tide. A family of six had to wade for it when I was there last. It is also open-ended and connects small beaches on either side of the headland, though perhaps the wizard used his skills to transform this unpromising habitation into a desirable residence.

SLAUGHTERBRIDGE

A short drive from Tintagel, a mile upriver from the town of Camelford, is Slaughterbridge, the legendary scene of Arthur's last battle. It is an ancient stone bridge stretching low and flat over the infant River Camel which usually chatters shallowly among pebbles and kingcups. On one of the days I visited it however floods had raised the level of the stream so much that it had almost submerged

Slaughterbridge: 'legendary scene of Arthur's last battle.'▶

▼Arthur's Grave: 'an eerie dignity and significance.'

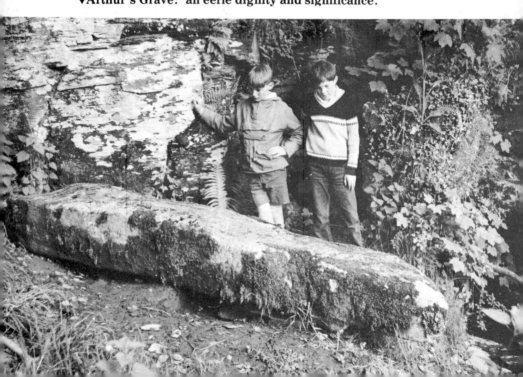

'To me Dozmary has always been the most
beautiful and eerie part of the moor.'

two fallen tree-trunks which usually make effective fords. I ended
up with muddy feet and wet legs, so be warned and take wellingtons
when you go.

Half-hidden among the trees beside the Camel, a few yards
upstream, lies a great stone called Arthur's grave, but more likely
the monument to another Celtic chieftain, slain in an historic battle
fought in 825 during the Saxon conquest of Cornwall. The first time
I found the stone, after clambering down a slippery bank and
inching along the fern-draped stones at the edge of the stream, the
frisson of discovery was strong. It remains so on all later visits,
particularly at dusk when the great slab, encrusted with moss and
faintly etched by man and weather with strange runnels, takes on
an eerie dignity and significance. It is a stark memorial, worthy of a
king, even if many people believe that Arthur himself rests
elsewhere 'in Avalon, with the fairest of all women'.

The historical facts and doubts cannot detract from the stirring quality of the accounts of Arthur's last battle. My favourite is the description by the twelfth century priest, Layamon, in his Middle English poem, the *Historia Brutonum*, or *Brut*:

> *On the River Camel, they came together*
> *The place was called Camelford. May the name last forever*
> *And at Camelford were gathered sixty thousand*
> *And more. Modred was their leader.*
> *And the noble Arthur rode there*
> *With a huge army, although it was doomed.*
> *On the River Camel, they fought together,*
> *Raised standards, massed them together,*
> *Drew long swords and beat on the helmets.*
> *Sparks flew out, spears shattered*
> *Shields broke, shafts snapped*
> *The mighty host fought together there.*
> *The Camel was in flood with measureless blood.*

Somehow the heroic brevity communicates the battle's epic quality far more tellingly than any number of fulsome tales of feats of arms.

DOZMARY POOL

From Slaughterbridge, I travelled east to Dozmary Pool, set high and mysterious on Bodmin Moor. It lay like a mirror in the austere landscape, deep sky resting on the sheet of moorland and magic pool below, broad horizontal lines broken only by the occasional clump of reeds or withered thorn bush. To me Dozmary has always been the most beautiful and eerie part of the moor, fed by no obvious streams or springs but appearing naturally in the windswept natural basin.

The legends are an organic part of the scene. The least imaginative would invent them if the lake were not already haunted by the ghosts of Tregeagle and Sir Bedivere who after some controversy, returned Arthur's great sword Excalibur to the Lady of the Lake. Bedivere carried the dying Arthur away after the Battle of Camlann, and the King ordered him to throw Excalibur into the nearby pool. Bedivere took the sword and hid it, then returned to his master who asked him what he had seen. 'Nothing except the ripples on the lake,' said Bedivere. The King was furious and raged at the knight for deceiving him, commanding him to take the sword again and carry out his orders to the letter. Bedivere again went away and again hid Excalibur, thinking it a terrible waste to throw the bejewelled weapon away. When he returned to Arthur with the same story as before, the King was more furious than ever and threatened to hurl Excalibur into Dozmary himself and then kill Bedivere with his bare hands, in spite of his dreadful wounds. At this Bedivere realised that his mission had a deeper, mystical significance than he had imagined so he did as he was told and, in the simple prose of Malory, 'threw the sword into the water as far as he might, and there came an arm and a hand above the water and met it and caught it, and so shook it thrice and brandished. And then the hand vanished away with the sword in the water.'

So the sword which the Lady of the Lake had given Arthur, vanished into the deep again as mysteriously as it had come.

Many people used to believe that Dozmary was bottomless, and perhaps the legends of its enchantment discouraged anyone from proving this wrong until recently. The first time I visited it, a herd of cows were standing up to their shoulders in water near the centre, so still that they were reflected perfectly in the lake like a band of hippos. I later met a man who claimed to have waded right across, without even getting his hair wet. All the same he believed the stories of Tregeagle and King Arthur implicitly, his Faith unshaken even though he had proved one detail wrong.

WICKED TREGEAGLE

Another name inevitably associated with Dozmary Pool is that of Jan Tregeagle, the evil steward of Lanhydrock. The storms howling across Bodmin Moor still hold a sinister note for country people, more chilling than the iciest north wind. Although Tregeagle has been in his grave four hundred years, they say that his black soul is doomed to wander for ever, howling in anguish at the heart of the tempest.

During his life, Jan Tregeagle must have booked a seat in the hottest part of hell. He murdered his first wife and children, then married a succession of heiresses, killing each in turn for her money.

26

He stole the estates of an orphan and grew rich on the gains of his dishonest stewardship. To round off a full-bodied life of crime, he sold his soul to the Devil, which seems a superfluous transaction considering his previous record, though perhaps he needed the money. According to an early nineteenth century ballad by John Penwarne, *Tregeagle or Dozmare Pool*, Tregeagle was a willing convert to Satan's fold:

> *A bargaine! A bargaine! then said he aloud,*
> *At my lot I will never repyne;*
> *I swear to observe it, I sweare by the roode,*
> *And am ready to seale and sygne with my bloode,*
> *Both my soule and my bodye are thyne.*

He evidently had second thoughts towards the end of his life and used some of his ill-gotten gains to bribe the clergy to bury him in the consecrated ground of St Breock churchyard. This had little

The Hermitage of Roche Rock

▲Loe Bar: 'one great sack which shed its load.'

Wicked Tregeagle: 'kept at his task by tormenting demons.'▶

effect, and shortly after his death, Tregeagle was called from the grave by a foolhardy debtor in court at Bodmin. The steward had been the only witness of a large loan made to the debtor by a money-lender. The debtor later denied all knowledge of the loan, certain that it could never be proved and when the case came to court, he rashly declared: 'Ef Tregeagle ever seed the money paid, may Tregeagle appear and declare et.' There was a flash of lightning and the ghost of Tregeagle appeared, seething with unearthly rage: 'Thee hast found et easy to bring me here,' he snarled, 'but thee west find et harder to put me away agen.'

With that, he hurled himself upon the terrified defendant, intent on tearing him limb from limb. Only the man's presence of mind saved his life, for he snatched up a newborn baby whose innocence served to ward off the evil spirit. He then employed a vicar to exorcise the ghost who was banished to Dozmary Pool on Bodmin

Moor, to empty this supposedly bottomless lake with a leaking limpet shell — Cornwall's answer to Sisyphus, everlastingly rolling his boulder uphill. He was kept at his task by tormenting demons until at the height of a terrifying storm, he cleared the lake with one huge bound and hurtled across the wastes of Bodmin to the hermitage of Roche Rock with the demons in hot pursuit. He stuck his head through the east window of the sanctuary in terror and stayed there, screaming, for two days before the priest moved him on to Padstow. He was no more welcome here and St Petroc banished him to Bareppa near Helston and told him to carry sacks of sand across the estuary of the River Cober and empty them at Porthleven. This he did until his hounding demons made him drop one great sack which shed its load in the river, forming Loe Bar.

Some say he became a huge bird, luring travellers to their deaths on Bodmin Moor, others that he now swoops around the cliffs of Land's End as a giant gull. In another version, he was finally set to weave a truss of sand at Gwenvor Cove, where he still battles vainly with the north wind which comes to destroy his work, howling in rage until the end of time.

ST NEOT

From Dozmary, I drove through wooded lanes the four miles to the peaceful village of St Neot, home of perhaps the most endearing saint of all.

'There are more saints in Cornwall than there are in heaven,' runs a Cornish saying, which leads the logical to wonder where the others ended up. Certainly they are a mixed bunch, some holy and learned, but others given to decidedly unsaintly actions. St Neot definitely belonged to the former category. He possessed the enchanting gift of charming animals and when a farmer complained that a flock of crows were destroying his corn, he miraculously impounded the birds until the harvest was over. On another occasion, his team of oxen was stolen so wild oxen gathered and meekly offered their necks to the yoke.

One day an angel appeared to St Neot and showed him three fish in his pond, promising the saint that if he ate only one fish each day, the supply would never run out. All went well until St Neot fell ill and his servant, perhaps thinking that his master needed extra

St Neot's Church

protein, caught two of the fish and cooked them. Neot was horrified when he discovered the mistake and ordered the servant to throw both fish back in the pond at once. He prayed to God for forgiveness and sure enough, the fish came back to life and swam around as if nothing had happened.

The Saint's life is vividly illustrated by a fifteenth century stained glass window in St Neot Church, showing the most striking episodes in a series of lively pictures. The church is well worth a visit, both for the Saint's sake and for the rarity of the windows, since it is the only Cornish church which still boasts the greater part of its original pre-Reformation stained glass. When I visited the church, a class of school-children were clustered around the St Neot window, disentangling the various tales and identifying the different animals which are portrayed with a charmingly earnest simplicity.

THE HURLERS

A short distance east of St Neot, I followed the signposts to the Hurlers, three interlocking rings of standing stones set in the stark landscape of Bodmin Moor, near the tiny village of Minions. They hold an intangible power, even for the casual tourist who strays the few hundred yards off the road to see them. Part of that power lies in their mixture of mystery and significance, for although the stones are placed with scientific precision, their centres lying along a straight line, no-one is entirely sure why they were erected or what strange ceremonies were enacted there long before the birth of Christianity.

Most of the stones in the middle circle are still standing, at regular intervals round central chunks of granite, much in the manner of men earnestly engaged in French cricket. In the outer rings, only a handful remain. A few lie where they have fallen, covered now in moss and heather, but the three groups still produce an eerie atmosphere with their hunched shapes and deliberate positions, so it is easy to believe the tradition that it is impossible to count them and arrive at the same number twice. I can vouch for the

Author with novelist, E.V. Thompson at The Hurlers▶

truth of the saying, for when I visited the Hurlers for the first time with a numerate and intelligent friend, we not only failed to reach the same number twice, but even disagreed when we counted round the circles together and compared totals.

The eighteenth century historian, William Borlase, believed them to be the Druid's temples and dismissed the popular legend with elegant scorn: 'The stones by the vulgar are supposed to have been once men and thus transformed as a punishment for their hurling upon the Lord's Day.' It is an explanation, however, which at least half-a-dozen of the older inhabitants of Minions swear is true.

According to all eye-witness accounts, hurling was a savage free-for-all in which men of rival villages vied to knock a ball through goals often placed several miles apart. The Bodmin hurlers evidently practised a particularly sedate version of the game in deference to the Sabbath. Or perhaps I was right after all and they *were* playing French cricket.

TRETHEVY QUOIT

Also signposted from the road between St Cleer and Minions is Trethevy or Arthur's Quoit. It is a magnificent monument to some high priestly family or dynasty of chieftains of the Megalithic era. Although today the smooth slab of the capstone rears obliquely from its cluster of upright supports, a striking, curiously elephantine piece of sculpture, high, grey and bulky, it would originally have been covered with a cairn mound at least to the level of the capstone. Removal of the cairn revealed two burial chambers formed by the uprights, giving the tomb great rarity value since Trethevy and Zennor are the only two surviving quoits in Cornwall with a second chamber.

I reached the inner tomb by crawling through a tiny aperture in the stone and later heard the three conflicting explanations for the narrow gap: the first, to allow the spirits of the dead to escape; the second, to allow food to be placed inside as sustenance through eternity; and the third, to prevent the spirits of the dead escaping. All three seem to me equally unlikely. If God or the Devil wants a

◄Trethevy Quoit: 'a striking, curiously elephantine piece of sculpture.'

▲The Bridle Lane from Talland Beach: '. . . stories
of satanic apparitions scared off prying excisemen.'▶

soul badly enough, 'stone walls do not a prison make', and no physical escape route is necessary either. As for the food, if heaven is half what it is cracked up to be, any soul that achieves it will tend to turn its spiritual nose up — in the saintliest way, of course — at any earthly edibles, however delicious. If, by contrast, the soul is condemned to everlasting torment, unable to touch the endless feasts set out to tantalise it unbearably, it would seem bad policy for the Devil to allow it supplies from home, just as a strict housemaster would confiscate tuck given to boys in detention.

No, my private theory is that the hole into the inner chamber is designed for the purely practical purpose of discouraging both grave robbers and, in later years, nosy sightseers like me.

ENTER THE DEVIL

From his brimstone bed at break of day,
A-walking the devil is gone,
To visit his snug little farm the earth
And see how his stock goes on.

Over the hill and over the dale
And he went over the plain,
And backward and forward he switched his long tail
As a gentleman switches his cane.

(Coleridge — The Devil's Thoughts)

If the Hurlers were the Lord's work, the Devil was still more active a few miles further south at Polperro, perhaps to counter all the Saints in Cornwall and add a little spice to the prevailing sanctity. A great rent in the slate formations behind the little town marks one spot where he burst through from the realms of darkness, his flaming chariot drawn by a jet-black steed. The huge beast reared and pawed the air, exhilarated by the wind in his mane. He planted his fiery hoof on the ground, shaking the region like an earthquake and striking sparks from the slate. The impact left behind an impression which survives to this day as a peculiar, hoof-shaped pool.

'The quiet estuary village of Lerryn.'▶

38

The Devil did not have all his own way on his jaunts into East Cornwall. In the eighteenth century, the famous ghost-laying parson, Richard Dodge, vicar of Talland near Polperro, put him to flight when he met him driving his black coach and headless horses. Reverend Dodge literally put the fear of God into the Devil who screeched: 'Dodge is come! I must be gone!' and vanished. Doubting Thomases of the vicar's flock remained sceptical about the exorcism and swore that Dodge was in league with the smugglers, using the stories of satanic apparations in the Bridle Lane leading from Talland Beach to scare off prying excisemen.

THE GIANT'S HEDGE

A few minutes' drive from Polperro, at the quiet estuary village of Lerryn, I discovered the Devil's most lasting feat of architecture, an earthwork whose origin is explained in the rhyme

The Devil having nothing to do,
Built a great wall from Lerryn to Looe.

He certainly did a thorough if pointless job, for many sections of the broad earthwork, confusingly known as the 'Giant's Hedge', are still visible between Lerryn and the coast. For many historians, it is merely a fortification built in the sixth century by the Cornish King Mark to repel the invading Irish, but true Cornishmen prefer the old theory of its satanic origin.

Surprisingly few people, even locals, knew of its existence when I investigated its whereabouts, and I drew a blank until the Lerryn farmer whose land it crosses gave me exact directions, including the great overhanging beech tree where a lane intersects it. Nowadays it is well-camouflaged by a thick covering of bracken, bushes and trees, so I felt a real thrill of discovery when I 'found' it for the first time, a wooded bank, eight yards wide and fifteen feet high in places, striding proudly alongside Ribby Wood, vanishing and then reappearing again, the broad, broken swathe clearly visible from most hilltops between Lerryn and Looe.

The Giant's Hedge:
'The Devil's most lasting feat of architecture.' ▶

40

THE PRIZE WRESTLER AND THE DEMON

Human contacts with the Devil are as common in legend as geographical reminders of his presence. In many stories, the Devil appears in disguise, proposing a wager with a soul at stake. In most the rash mortals are carried off to hell in an enjoyably terrifying fashion, but a few miles west of Truro in the village of Ladock, I heard the story of a local boy who gave the Devil more than he bargained for.

The Ladock wrestler, Jacky Trevail, felt proud of his skill when he threw the champion of another parish one midsummer day, so proud that he declared: 'I'm open to a challenge from any man, in fact I wouldn't mind a bout with the Devil himself.' He made his way home slowly, and a little unsteadily, the result of drink and exhaustion. As he crossed a nearby common called Le Pens Plat, he met a man dressed like a vicar, who congratulated him on his great victory and asked him for a contest, wagering five guineas to Jacky's prize, a magnificent gold-laced hat. The stranger insisted that they fight at midnight because it would never do for his parishioners to see him wrestling in broad daylight. Jacky agreed, so they arranged to meet the following night at midnight. The vicar handed over his five guinea wager, but as they shook hands to seal the bargain, Jacky caught sight of a cloven hoof under the vicar's cassock. He made his way home in fear and trembling, convinced he had sold his soul to the Devil.

The following day, he told the whole story to the local parson, Mr Wood, who advised him to carry out his part of the bargain but keep a scrap of paper bearing mystical signs and words next to his heart. Jacky did as he was told, and at midnight, he and his mysterious opponent started wrestling, the stranger getting the best of it at first, seizing Jacky by his waistband and rising above the earth with him until the Ladock lad thought it was all over with him. All the same, he struggled valiantly and when his waistcoat touched the 'parson', the strange man fell to the ground, writhing like a wounded snake.

The Evil One — for by now his true identity was obvious — sprang to his feet, shouting, 'You have some concealed weapon about ye that has wounded me. Cast off that waistcoat!' but Jacky refused and they struggled for five long minutes at arm's length.

Eventually the parson was thrown again and lay flat on his back, belching out brimstone fumes. He sprang up again, more furious than ever and said: 'In the name of fair play, tell Parson Wood to go home. I'm confused and powerless while he's looking on, for I can see his eyes gleaming at me behind that hedge and he is mumbling something to himself.

'Take no notice,' said Jacky, 'Parson Wood can wrestle very well himself and likes to see a good contest.' At that, he picked up his opponent in a Cornish Hug and flattened him a third time, then stood over him in case he wanted some more punishment. The sky became very dark, clouds covered the moon and in the dim light, the defeated wrestler writhed, more snake-like than ever. Then his feet turned into the claws of a huge bird, his skirts became a pair of wings and he was transformed into a dragon. The great beast flew off into the gathering clouds, leaving a path of flame in his wake, and as he entered the blackest cloud of all, it revolved in the air like an immense wheel, sending out forked lightning and thunder bolts.

On the ground below, Jacky was still gathering his wits when Parson Wood put a hand on his shoulder and pointed to where a streak of fire from the cloud shot down the sky and fell in the next parish of St Enoder.

'There's your wrestling Devil, Jacky,' said the parson. We haven't seen the last of him yet. I was on the ground long before midnight and summoned many powerful spirits to guard you and watch the contest — and a fine one it was too.'

Jacky thanked Parson Wood heartily for saving his life and promised to serve him day and night. He remained the prize-wrestler of Ladock for many years but he never again made a pact with the Devil.

ST MAWES

From the wooded, marshy land around Ladock, I made my way to St Mawes, opposite Falmouth. The Saint who gave the town its name must have possessed a testy disposition and he evidently abhorred any disruption of his ministry, for when a noisy seal interrupted his sermon with its barking and braying, he flew into an uncontrollable rage and raised a great boulder above his head, hurling it at the beast with all his might. It must have been a prodigious throw, because the boulder missed but remains perched on the Black Rocks in Falmouth Harbour, where it is visible at low tide, signalled by a conical marker. The chair from which the Saint had been preaching is likewise preserved, set into the wall of a St Mawes house.

ST KEVERNE

Lizard country is the most southerly land in Britain. Although St Keverne in this heel of Cornwall is only a few miles south of St Mawes, the landscapes are vastly different. The Saints who give the places their names, however, shared an irascible temperament with few of the saintly virtues such as tolerance or forgiveness.

Piqued by the local people's lack of respect for him, St Keverne declared that no metal would ever ring within the sound of his bells. Certainly the deposits of tin and copper which have enriched Cornwall are conspicuously absent from the Lizard peninsula.

Even Keverne's friends betrayed his hospitality, for when St Just walked over from Penwith to have supper with him, he spent the meal coveting a bejewelled chalice belonging to his host. Before he set out on his homeward journey, Just slipped the cup onto his belt then strode off across the moor. When St Keverne noticed his loss, he chased St Just, throwing stones at him from Crousa Down, but 'St Just was too deeply absorbed in religious meditation to notice' and kept running as if unaware of the huge chunks of stone falling around him. Eventually the boulders got too close for comfort, so St Just undid the chalice and dropped it behind him. Keverne picked it up and returned home, but until the last century, the stones lay where they had fallen in a field near Germoe, providing a riddle for geologists, for they were unlike any occurring naturally round there, but identical to a type of gritstone found on Crousa Down.

At least in his treatment of animals, St Keverne showed a little more patience, for when two birds built a nest in his hands, as he prayed, he refused to change his position until the chicks had hatched. A case of going to work on an egg?

St Keverne's Church: 'no metal would ring within sound of his bells.' ▶

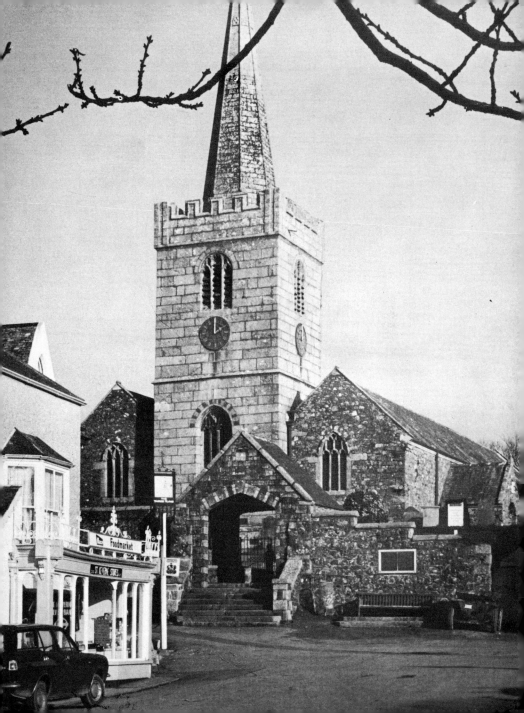

ST PIRAN

St Piran must have seemed too good for this world to the rough and heathen Irish he tried to convert. They tired of his good deeds and threw him into a stormy sea, tied to a millstone which, instead of dragging the Saint to a watery death, floated and carried him over the waves, now miraculously stilled, to the sandy beach of Perranzabuloe which means 'St Piran in the sands'. Here he built a little oratory, where his first disciples are said to have been a badger, a bear and a fox. The tiny cell was unearthed in the nineteenth century after being inundated by sand for hundreds of years. A line of white stones now leads to the site of the oratory, a mile off the Perranporth road. When I trekked there over the undulating sands, it was easy to imagine myself a pilgrim in search of St Piran. In early autumn, the sandy hills were empty of tourists and a ceaseless wind shook the spiky grass and sea-holly. Nearby dunes are still crowned with standing stones and ancient crosses, and the bright blustery day did nothing to dispel the awesome sense of sanctity I felt in that deserted place.

Disappointingly, I found the remains of the oratory hidden by a concrete building like a large air-raid shelter, erected to prevent their total destruction by vandals, and now, itself in danger of collapse. Feeling like a schoolboy scrumping apples, and ignoring the warnings, I climbed onto the roof of the shelter and peered through a narrow slit, desperate for even a glimpse of the interior. Once my eyes became accustomed to the semi-darkness, I could faintly see the remains of a stone wall at the far end, and a pile of debris, half-covered in wet sand. I reflected that after so many centuries, the relic's very survival was amazing. At present, its future is in doubt. Some groups are in favour of allowing it to return beneath the sand, marked by a commemorative cross above it, others wish to incorporate the remains into a Cornish Saints' museum. Whatever happens, the destruction of the unsightly shed that houses it is guaranteed, unless it first falls down of its own accord, crushing nearby vandals and foolhardy writers alike.

One faction has even tried to revive the oratory as a place of

◀St Piran's Oratory: 'I found the remains ... hidden by a concrete building like a large air-raid shelter.'

pilgrimage, its function in the Middle Ages when relics of St Piran were highly prized and thousands of believers would visit his shrine each year. Even today, the bleak, windswept surroundings give an overwhelming impression of Piran's austere life and cramped conditions made all the more uncomfortable by his great height, for a huge skeleton discovered near Perranzabuloe is said to be his.

According to tradition, St Piran, the patron saint of tinners, actually discovered tin when he used a large black stone for his fireplace. As the flames became hotter, he noticed in amazement that a stream of pure white metal was trickling from the stone. He shared his find with the local people who were so delighted at their new-found prosperity that they held a sumptuous feast where the ale and wine ran like water, a fact which St Piran no doubt appreciated for he was a great tippler and is said to have died drunk at the age of 206. The debauch is still commemorated today in the local phrase 'As drunk as a Perraner' and the Cornish Nationalists, Mebyon Kernow, have adopted a white cross on a black background, representing white tin on black base rock, as their standard.

GIANT BOLSTER

Tall as he was, St Piran would have been dwarfed by the huge, shambling figure of Giant Bolster who was so immense that it was said he could plant one foot in Carn Brea and the other in St Agnes, six miles away as the crow flies. Like most giants, the size of his emotions matched his stature: quarrels became blood-feuds, anger turned to violent rage, and when he fell in love with the virtuous St Agnes, the depth of his devotion must have been intensely embarrassing, particularly since she was sworn to chastity and he was both ugly and uncouth. He used to follow her around, asking only to be near her, but hoping against hope that she would return his love.

Eventually she could bear it no longer and devised a most unsaintly scheme to rid herself of his attentions. Pretending at last to take him seriously she commanded him to prove his love for her

Giant Bolster: '... plunged a knife into a vein.'▶

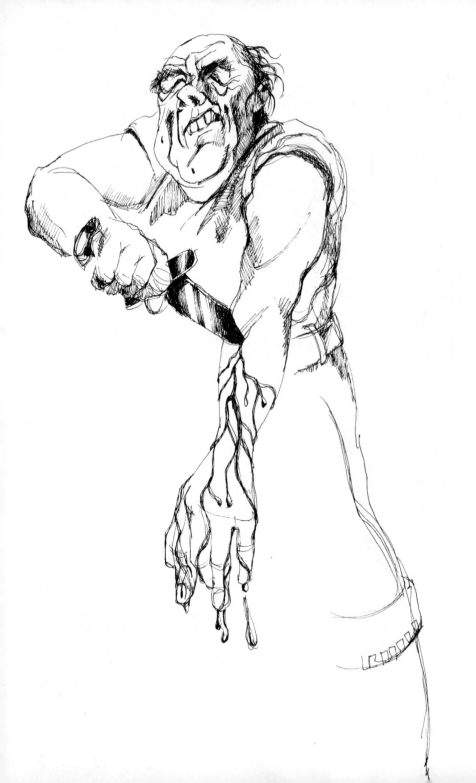

by filling a hole in the cliff at Chapel Porth with his blood, knowing full well that the hole was bottomless and led into the sea below. The Giant gladly assented, thinking that he would scarcely miss the small amount of blood needed to fill the hole. Stretching out his arm, he plunged a knife into the vein so that the blood gushed out, then lay down and waited for the hole to fill up. Of course it was all in vain, and although at first he was rather surprised that it was taking such a long time, he soon felt too faint from loss of blood to know what was happening and eventually died, murmuring St Agnes' name. The cliffs at Chapel Porth still bear a red stain where his blood ran down into the sea.

THE GIANT WRATH OF PORTREATH

The seas around North Cornwall are notoriously dangerous, 'a watery grave by day and night', so it is easy to see the origin of legends like the one about the clifftop monster whose staple diet was well-fed sailors. The Giant known as Wrath of Portreath lived up to his name in a ferocious manner. He lived in a cavern which is now called Ralph's Cupboard. Since his death, it has lost its roof and has become the open gorge it is today with the sea flowing in at high tide.

The fearful Wrath used to lie in wait for any St Ives ships or fishing boats which sailed near his lair. If they passed within a mile, he would wade out, and braining the sailors with his club-like fingers he would tie the ships to his belt and stride back, pulling them behind him. Once home, he kept the plump young men, without too much gristle and sinew, in his larder but the lean ones he threw back in the sea.

Even ships sailing in deeper water were not safe from him, for he sunk many by slinging rocks on them from the cliff. These rocks are still visible at low tide and form the dangerous reef stretching from Godrevy Head. Even after the Giant's death his cupboard remained a place of terror which the St Ives fishermen avoided at all costs, swearing that nothing ever came out of it that had the misfortune to be drawn in.

◀'The cliffs at Chapel Porth still bear a red stain.'

THE MUTTON FEAST AT ST IVES

The cliffs of Cornwall also played a part in a 'misfortune' which befell a farmer near St Ives. Not everybody considered it a misfortune though, more a case of 'one man's mutton is another man's mackerel'. Accustomed to a repetitive diet of 'scads and tates and conger' — oily mackerel, potatoes and conger eel — the fishermen of St Ives held a joyful feast in the Middle Ages after what they considered a miraculous catch. A flock of sheep grazing on the slopes of neighbouring Gwithian were blown into the sea during a frightful storm and hauled up along with the mackerel and pilchards.

In 1800, the poet Fortescue Hitchin recounted the ancient tale, describing the delight of the fishermen with great gusto:

> *With joy they see the mutton store*
> *And 'heava' sound from shore to shore.*

Heva was the shout of the clifftop watchers at the approach of the pilchard shoals. Hitchin treats the little matter of conscience tongue-in-cheek:

> *So counting honestly the sheep*
> *A Godsend from the stormy deep,*
> *All hands turned to with wondrous pain*
> *To share the unexpected gain.*

Scruples aside, all's well that ends well:

> *Now those who had to feed on fish*
> *Ten minutes took to enjoy that dish,*
> *An hour now to dinner linger*
> *To pick the bones and lick the finger.*

◀Ralph's Cupboard: '. . . a place of terror.'

▲St Michael's Mount: 'the fairytale castle.'▶

ST MICHAEL'S MOUNT

Taking a detour southwards to Marazion, the great sweep of Mount's Bay unfolded and I caught my first magical glimpse of St Michael's Mount, the fairytale castle separated from the mainland by a causeway covered at high tide. Today the Mount must attract more sightseers than any other beauty-spot in Cornwall, a far cry from the days when visitors ran the risk of being crushed like flies by huge cobbling hammers thrown in sport.

It is said that the Mount was called after St Michael because he appeared in a vision to a group of fishermen, while in another version, the Saint appeared to a hermit of the Mount.

Years before the vision, the Giant Cormoran built the Mount to provide himself with a home and a vantage point where he could watch the surrounding countryside. As in many families the Giant carefully selected the building materials, pale chunks of quartz from

the neighbouring hills, but left his wife, Cormelian, to do much of the heavy manual work. She toiled to and fro in the hot sun, dutifully carrying the huge masses in her apron on the long journey from the hills to the Mount which was nearing completion and had earned itself the Cornish name of *Carrek Los y'n Cos* — 'the grey rock in the wood' — because of its unusual colour. However this cut little ice with the exhausted Cormelian who merely wanted to finish her task as quickly as possible. Noticing an outcrop of greenstone nearby, she saw no reason why this should not do as well as the granite, so waiting until Cormoran was asleep, she broke off a great chunk and hurried towards the Mount, carrying it in her apron. The Giant woke up and noticing her substitution of green rock for grey, flew into such a rage that he swore dreadfully and kicked her hard. Her apron string broke and the greenstone fell onto the causeway where it has remained ever since. It is now known as Chapel Rock because of the 'Lytle chapel' built there during the Dark Ages.

Cormelian met her death accidentally when a cobbling hammer thrown by the Giant of Trecobben — now Trencrom Hill — smashed her skull. Both Giants were desolated, even the rough-and-ready Cormoran, and they sorrowfully buried her body beneath Chapel Rock, the Giant of Trecobben Hill eventually dying of grief and remorse. He left his treasure buried deep among the cairns of Trecobben where it still lies in glittering heaps, guarded by troops of fierce soldier-elves called spriggans.

LEGENDS OF THE MINES

Just as the Giant's gold was put under guard, so too, according to tradition was tin, the natural treasure found so abundantly both in Penwith and the rest of Cornwall. St Piran's discovery of the precious metal had brought wealth for the few and work for the many, first in the streams and then in the mines of Cornwall, and a whole series of legends grew up around the tinners and copper-miners at their hard, dangerous and often frightening work.

Conditions as late as 1860 were so appalling that the life-expectancy of the St Cleer copper-miners was only 21. It was estimated that one in five died from accidents, but the damp, smoke-sodden air was an even greater killer and more than half the men died from the chest complaints it caused. Richard Couch, a

Dolcoath Mine: '. . . **hard dangerous** and often frightening work.'

mine-surgeon from St Austell, described the tinners' physical condition: 'To see the men arriving at surface after eight hours work is a most sickening sight. Thin, haggard, with arms apparently very much lengthened and hanging almost uselessly by their sides, they seem like men worn out rather than tired.' Few mines boasted even the simplest form of lift so the men faced the added strain of climbing down two thousand feet of ladders to reach the mine face. It took three quarters of an hour to go down to the face and twice the time on the return journey after the shift was over.

In the face of this unimaginable hardship, it is easy to see why the mystique and myths of their trade were so precious to the tinners. Most were superstitious and believed implicitly in the existence of the spirits who haunted the mines — knockers, or nuggies. It was a brave man who did not leave a morsel of crust from his pasty to placate them. Even today, swearing and whistling underground are considered unlucky in case they annoy the spirits, and many miners have an aversion to the sign of the cross because the knockers were thought to be either the ghosts of the Jews who crucified Jesus or the souls of those too good for hell but too bad for heaven.

They were usually described as small, withered creatures with large ugly heads and the faces of old men. As they only worked on rich lodes, they could be very useful, but needed careful handling as they were capricious and could be very spiteful if crossed, as many tinners found to their cost.

BARKER'S KNEE

One miner who dismissed the knockers as mere superstition carried the mark of his scepticism for the rest of his life. He was a lazy man named Barker who, after long arguments with his fellow tinners about the existence of the knockers, went to a nearby mine and lay in wait for them at the top of the shaft. After a time he heard the little creatures whispering and chattering below him, and found out that, like the human tinners, they worked eight hour shifts, then hid their tools near the head of the mine. Barker decided to steal the tools if he could discover their hiding place, so he listened more

Barker's Knee: '. . . he walked with a limp until his dying day.'▶

'The mystique and myths of their trade were precious to the tinners . . .'

carefully, never guessing that the knockers knew he was there and hated being spied on.

'I shall leave my tools at the bend in the stream,' said one. 'I shall leave mine under the bramble bush,' said another. The third laughed evilly: 'And I shall leave mine on Barker's Knee.' Barker screamed as a huge weight smashed down on his left knee and unearthly, mocking laughter rang in his ears. He never poured scorn on the knockers again, but all the same he walked with a limp until his dying day.

TOM TREVORROW

Another tinner, Tom Trevorrow from St Just, doubted the power of the *bucca* — a Cornish word for imp which has passed obliquely into English as 'bug-a-boo', a frightening apparition, from the Cornish *bucca dhu*, black imp. Tom was working in the Ballowal Mine when he heard the knockers, but instead of showing them any respect, he

'. . . superstition and belief in ghosts existed quite naturally.'

told them to go away. Even a hail of small stones left him unmoved and he went on working until the sprites whispered to him:

> *Tom Trevorrow! Tom Trevorrow!*
> *Leave some of thy fuggan for bucca*
> *Or bad luck to thee tomorrow.*
> (*Fuggan* is a heavy Cornish lardy-cake.)

Tom took no notice: 'Go to blazes, you cussed old Jews' sperrats or I'll scat ye brains out!'
The knockers spoke again, their voices loud and threatening:

> *Tommy Trevorrow! Tommy Trevorrow!*
> *We'll send thee bad luck tomorrow,*
> *Thou old curmudgeon to eat all thy fuggan*
> *And not leave a didjan for Bucca.*
> (A *didjan* means a little piece.)

After that, nothing prospered with Tom and soon afterwards his precious tools were buried in a rock-fall which also covered the lode of rich ore he had been working. He struggled on, hoping his luck would turn, but in the end, his misfortunes piled up. He was forced to leave the mine and become a farm-labourer, a most inferior occupation for a tinner.

GHOSTS OF THE MINES

For the tinners, superstition and belief in ghosts existed quite naturally alongside the fervent Methodism which the Wesleys spread through Cornwall after their initial, apathetic reception in 1743. Some of the apparitions spelt doom and in many mines a disembodied hand carrying a tallow candle or clutching the rung of the ladder directly above a descending miner foretold disaster for him that day.

At Polbreen Mine, the ghost of Dorcas, an old woman who had thrown herself down a shaft, usually played tricks on the tinners, calling them by name to lure them from their work, or tearing the shirts from their backs. One day, however, she saved a man from certain death. Two miners were at work in Darkey's (Dorcas's) shaft when one heard his name called more and more insistently. He dropped his tools and ran to see who was looking for him. Seconds later, a massive rock-fall crashed down onto the spot where he had been working.

At Wheal Vor, a white hare was considered a fatal omen and many miners would never mention certain animals by name, but invented secret descriptive phrases for them: a hare was a 'long ear', an owl a 'braced farcer' and a rat a 'peep'.

TRENWITH'S BARGAIN

Ransom Mine was reputed to be alive with knockers. The clicks of their little picks sounded through each level, but most of all at the

◀ **Bucca: '... small, withered, with a large ugly head and the face of an old man.'**

63

one known as Bockles, and everyone believed that the richest rewards of all were here for the taking. None of them dared to work at Bockles, however, for fear of offending the knockers.

An old man called Trenwith went out with his son one night at midnight and saw the little men lugging out great heaps of the shining metal so, greatly daring, the humans struck up a bargain with them, that in exchange for being allowed to work the lode, they would leave one tenth, properly prepared, to save the knockers the trouble. Throughout his life the old man stuck strictly to his bargain and prospered accordingly, for in spite of leaving a tenth of the ore as he had promised, he still earned twice the money of any other tinner. After his death, his son continued to work at Bockles but he was selfish and grasping and stopped leaving any ore for the knockers. They soon showed their displeasure, for the lode failed and the son took to drink, eventually squandering all his father's fortune and dying a pauper.

TOWEDNACK CHURCH

From the Mount, a short journey through the Penwith Hills brought me to the picturesque and much-loved church of Towednack. Nearly everyone I spoke to named it as their favourite Cornish church, but its atmosphere of calm belies an eventful history, for its plain, squat tower remains a proof of Satan's destructiveness to this day. When the masons were building the tower of Towednack Church, the Devil came under cover of darkness and stole the battlements and pinnacles. Each time the work was renewed, he destroyed it again until the builders gave up in despair, swearing it was pointless to contend with Old Nick. That is why the tower still stands, lonely and stark and why, hopefully rather than justly, the locals quote a proverb that runs:

'There are no cuckolds in Towednack because there are no horns on the church tower.'

◄ The ghost of Dorcas: 'an old woman who had thrown herself down a shaft.'

▲Towednack Church: 'no cuckolds in Towednack . . .'

'. . . the Devil stole the battlements and pinnacles.'▶

TOWEDNACK CUCKOO FEAST

Although many people associate the cuckolds of this saying with the famous Towednack Cuckoo Feast, there is no actual connection as the feast dates back to pre-Christian times. A Towednack man was splitting logs at the end of the long bleak winter. Suddenly a cuckoo flew out, unharmed and calling joyously from the thick branch he had just chopped in half. The bird's arrival was taken as a good omen for the rest of the year and the whole village held a great feast to honour the cuckoo and to welcome the spring. Each year, on the nearest Sunday to 28 April, the people of Towednack still celebrate the event with the Cuckoo Feast, though only after they have heard the first notes of the cuckoo.

THE MERMAID OF ZENNOR

From Towednack, the coast road led me along the grassy slopes inclining steeply and smoothly down from the quoit-littered heights on my left to the sea, calm and Aegean-blue on my right — a view so breathtaking that I almost crashed the car while gazing over my shoulder. My next destination, Zennor Church, shares both Towednack's vicar and its charm. It is set high up, overlooking the sea, which was the home of the village's most famous character, the Mermaid of Zennor.

Mermaids appear in the legends of Cornwall, even before the dawn of Christianity, when they were one of the symbols of Aphrodite, the goddess of love, and held a quince — or love apple — and a comb. Later these became a mirror and a comb, symbols of heartlessness, since mermaids were supposed to lure men beneath the waves with their beautiful siren-like voices. In the Middle Ages, the symbol of the mermaid was used in the Cornish Mystery plays to explain the

◀ The Author on horseback: view from the saddle.

▼ Zennor Churchtown from John Wesley's stone.

**The Mermaid of Zennor: 'immortalised rather unflatteringly' on a
carved bench-end in Zennor Church.**

two natures of Christ: just as the mermaid is half-human, half-fish, so Christ is half-man, half-God.

Zennor's mermaid is immortalised, rather unflatteringly, on a carved bench-end in the little church which I visited at Harvest Festival. The church, bench-end and all, was glorious with flowers and fruit and wheatsheaf loaves, with only a smattering of tinned foods to set the seasonal scene in the twentieth century. The carved mermaid is estimated to be between five and six hundred years old and carries a comb and a glass. The dramatic story tells of how a strange and beautiful woman enchanted generations of Zennor churchgoers with her changeless loveliness and sweet voice. No-one knew her name or where she lived as she seemed to vanish after each service, only reappearing the following Sunday. Her beauty and mysterious air discouraged anyone from asking who she was and where she came from.

One day, she met Mathy Trewhella, the churchwarden's son. He was a handsome young man with the finest voice for miles around, and the Zennor church choir greatly missed him when he and the mysterious lady fell in love and left the district. Their fate remained a mystery until a few years later when a beautiful mermaid appealed to the captain of a ship anchored off Pendower Cove: 'Your anchor is blocking our cave and Mathy and our children are trapped inside.' The captain lifted anchor and sailed into St Ives. Soon the town was humming with the extraordinary event. For the people of Zennor the mystery was solved.

THE GIANT OF CARN GALVER

Above Zennor, the stone outcrops stand starkly at the edge of the high moors, balanced one upon another in strange shapes which make it difficult to believe they are really natural formations. No wonder the local people thought them the playthings of creatures like the Giant of Carn Galver of affectionate memory.

Unlike most of the Cornish giants who were usually cruel and selfish and killed men like flies, the Giant of Carn Galver had an amiable reputation and the only death he caused almost broke his heart. Far from terrorising the neighbourhood, he took great care of the people of Morvah and Zennor and he balanced a Logan stone on the most westerly carn of the range where he sat watching over the villages below.

Best of all he liked playing bob-button with his great friend, a young man from Choon — or Chûn — whose quoit can still be seen nearby. It had been a thrilling contest and when it was time for his friend to go home, the Carn Galver Giant tapped him lightly on the head with the tips of his fingers, saying: 'Be sure to come again tomorrow my son and we will have a capital game of bob.' To his horror, the young man fell down at his feet, for the Giant's fingers had gone straight through his skull. Bottrell records how the Giant 'did his best to put the inside workings of his mate's head to rights and plugged up his finger-holes — but all to no purpose, for the young man was stone dead long before the Giant ceased doctoring his head'.

At this he set up a great bellow, rocking the corpse in his arms and crying: 'Oh, my son, my son! Why didn't they make the shell of thy noddle stronger. A es as plum (soft) as a piecrust, dough-baked and made too thin by the half. How shall I ever pass the time without thee to play bob and mop-and-heede (hide-and-seek).' It is said that the Giant of Carn Galver never laughed again, but pined away forlornly, dying years later of a broken heart.

THE REVELS ON THE GUMP

Westwards from Morvah, the Gump at St Just has long been known as a favourite spot for the fairies' masques and banquets. This belief is still widespread and several of the older people whose families have lived nearby for generations told me that their own grand-parents and great-grandparents swore that they themselves had seen the 'good people'. This title was perhaps designed to appease the fairies who were notoriously capricious, just as the Greeks nicknamed the ferocious Furies 'The Kindly Ones' to placate them.

Most people who caught sight of the fairies knew better than to let on, but as usual, one rash and greedy old man decided to try to outwit the small people and steal their fabled treasures. One moonlit night at harvest time, he made his way over the Gump until he heard wild, enchanting music which made him laugh one second and cry the next as its mood changed. There was no sign of anyone, either elf or mortal, and the old man became convinced that the music came from beneath the ground. Suddenly the hill before him opened with a crash of sound like a hundred orchestras playing an infinitely grand chord. Lights blazed from every leaf and tuft of grass and a host of soldier elves or spriggans, six feet tall, marched out of the hillside clearing the way for the revels and posting themselves on each of the surrounding hillocks to guard their Prince and Princess.

Next came a crowd of servants carrying dining tables, silver plates, gold drinking vessels, goblets cut out of the purest diamonds and platters and baskets crammed with meats and poultry, glazed exquisitely with flowers and leaves, cakes iced like fairy palaces, their pinnacles and turrets of marzipan, fruits cascading in waterfalls from many-layered filigree bowls, and jellies as richly coloured and translucent as the jewels around them, but even this spectacle could not compare with the sight of the countless thousands of tiny, gorgeously-dressed lords and ladies who crowded out of the hillside, singing exquisitely, in honour of their Prince and Princess. The royal pair, beautiful and bejewelled were carried out upon litters of gauze with great ceremony and seated in state on a mound on the Gump.

The feast began and the old man, intent on treasure, started crawling towards the high table, unaware that the spriggans had thrown invisible threads about him and watched him warily. Taking off his hat, he began lowering it over the Prince and Princess, but in an instant a shrill whistle peeped, and the whole brilliant scene vanished into total darkness and he found he could not move an inch. His body felt like a pincushion and tiny pinches bruised him from head to toe. A platoon of spriggans rolled him down the mound and chained him to the earth where he lay in agony, unable to speak or move. As an added punishment, one of the troop leapt onto his nose and stamped up and down, laughing uproariously and shouting:

'Away, away, I smell the day!'

At that, the old man found himself alone but still unable to move. It was not until daybreak that he managed to move at last and found that his bonds had become myriad gossamer cobwebs winking with dewdrops.

He slunk off, cold and ashamed, and it was many months before his friends managed to winkle out of him how he had spent his night on the Gump.

74

THE MEN-AN-TOL

Retracing my way from St Just to Morvah, I took the road inland towards Madron and after a short run, found the well-worn footpath, conveniently signposted like many of the legendary sites, leading a mile over the moors to the upright pillars flanking the stone known as Men-an-Tol — stone with a hole. Even today it is still credited with healing powers and mothers of sickly children continue the old tradition of dragging them through the narrow hole in the centre stone 'nine times against the sun' to cure them of scrofula and rickets. Adult sufferers are not neglected either, and anyone with lumbago or sciatica should crame — crawl — on all fours round the central stone, then creep through the hole, quite a feat of agility as it is only a few inches above the ground. I tried it, having refused a second helping of pudding to ensure that I could squeeze through, then discovered a large puddle on either side. All the same, I have suffered no back trouble since, so perhaps it is worth the struggle and the wet knees!

Men-an-Tol: '. . . still credited with healing powers.'

▲Over the moors to Men-an-Tol. Ding Dong Mine in the background.
Men Scryfa: 'thought to be the burial place of a king.'▶

THE MEN SCRYFA

This part of Penwith is so heavy with history and legend that at
times the farms and cottages of today seem dwarfed by their
backcloth — a landscape where in times past mighty dramas,
human and supernatural, were played out, whose echoes and traces
now remain 'stamped on these lifeless things'.

A short walk beyond the Men-an-Tol stands the Men Scryfa —
inscribed stone — which is thought to be the burial place of a king
slain in the battle of Gendhal Moor. The pillar bears the words
Rialobrani Cunovali Fili — Rialobran son of Cunoval. Tradition has
it that the King stood nine feet tall, the same height as the pillar, and
that he lies beneath with all his arms and treasures.

By now the survival of these relics seems exceedingly unlikely for
so many men believed that a crock of gold was buried there that the
pillar fell down after illegal excavations. It lay unheeded for many

76

years until in 1862 the Antiquarian Society replaced it in its rightful position over the warrior's grave.

LANYON QUOIT

Half a mile from the Men-an-Tol, along the road to Madron stands Lanyon Quoit, a spectacular stone chamber-tomb resembling a giant table. A massive, flat capstone is supported by three smaller pillars to create one of the largest and most perfect quoits in England. It is easy to see why it was said to be the plaything of the local giants in their games of bob-button and why a group of Saxon kings are thought to have used it for a dining table.

According to legend, King Arthur, too, dined there on the eve of his last battle, and Merlin prophesied that the King and his chieftains would gather there again just before the end of the world.

JENNY AND THE CHANGELING

Continuing along the road to Penzance, it sometimes seems as if every field contains a standing stone or other relic, and the legends of the area are equally numerous. From the abundance of tales about them, the fairies, spriggans, witches and knockers of Penwith must once have outnumbered the human population by at least five to one. Many of the country people believed that they stole babies, leaving behind their own misshapen offspring in their place. A regular plea of Medieval baby-batterers was that their own child had been taken and that they were merely punishing the changeling to persuade it to go back to elfland.

One down-to-earth story tells of how a spriggan, a married man with a family, took the place of a poor woman's child one night while she was working late in the harvest fields near Penzance. When she came home, the mother, Jenny Trayer, was surprised to find the child out of the cradle and crawling in the corner where the faggots for the fire were piled. Too exhausted to notice much, she put the child back to bed and slept soundly herself. From that day, however, she had no more peace from the baby who previously used to lie all day gurgling happily to itself. Now it cried continually to be suckled and played with and overnight it lost its pink plumpness and big,

**Lanyon Quoit: 'King Arthur dined there on
the eve of his last battle.'**

blue eyes and looked a scrawny, staring, sallow-complexioned
creature.

Jenny Trayer at once suspected that it was a changeling and when
she told the neighbours, they advised her to dip it in Chapel Uny
Well on the first three Wednesdays in May. This she did, even
trudging off on the third Wednesday in spite of a blustery gale
which her perverse brat seemed to enjoy most of all. On the way
home, a shrill voice screeched from nowhere:

'Tredrill! Tredrill! Thy wife and child greet thee well.'

The baby cackled like an old man and replied in a cracked voice:

*What care I for wife and child
When I ride on Dowdy's back to Chapel Well
And have got pap my fill.*

Horrified, Jenny returned home as quickly as possible and again
confided in the neighbours. They suggested stronger measures:
'Lay the small body upon the ashes pile and beat it well with a

broom, then lay it naked under a church stile. There leave it and keep it without sight and hearing until the turn of the night when, nine times out of ten, the thing will be taken away and the stolen child returned.'

Despite feeling horribly guilty at such ill-treatment, she did as they said and the child roared fit to burst. However, the heart-rending remedy soon produced the desired results. Next day she found her own lovely child under the stile, sleeping soundly in a little nest of dry straw, beautifully clean and swathed in a piece of fine, lavender-coloured chintz.

Jenny was overjoyed and never let the baby out of her sight again. All the same, like every child that has been with the fairies, it afterwards seemed different from other children, singing unknown songs to itself in a strange tongue and talking to people nobody else could see.

THE MERRY MAIDENS

West of Penzance, near Lamorna Cove at Boleigh, stands a circle of stones which, like the Hurlers in East Cornwall, are said to be petrified humans. In legend, the ring, known as the Merry Maidens, is the relic of a band of young girls turned to stone because they danced on the Lord's day. The two tall single stones nearby are the Pipers who played for them to dance.

One historical possibility, however, is almost equally romantic, for this was the site of the last great battle in the west when the Saxons led by King Aethelstan defeated King Howel and the Cornish army. The whole area was once marked with barrows and Bronze Age bones and ashes, and the Pipers are said to represent the rival kings surrounded by the bodies of those killed in battle.

THE LOGAN STONE

A few miles west of Lamorna, the most famous of Cornwall's many Logan stones sits balanced opposite Porthcurno. Like every Logan

◄Merry Maidens: 'a band of girls who danced on the Lord's Day.'

stone, 'a finger's weight can rock it, a man's strength cannot dislodge it'. This phenomenon explains why it was once the haunt of the St Levan witches who gathered there to brew up the storms they needed to bring them rich pickings from wrecked ships. Even now some say that any woman who touches the stone nine times at midnight will become a witch. I have no wish to put this theory to the test for the stone still generates an eerie atmosphere.

In earlier centuries, it was used as a form of court for it was said that no criminal could make it rock. In 1824 a rowdy young Naval officer, Lieutenant Goldsmith, nephew of the poet, and twelve friends set out to disprove its famed immovability and eventually succeeded in pushing it from its perch to the beach below. If not criminals before this feat, they were certainly made to feel like criminals afterwards, and in the face of a furious public outcry, the Lieutenant was forced to pay £130 8s 6d to have the stone restored.

The details of payment are fascinating: John Berryman was paid three shillings a night as watchman and kept watch for 53 nights. Hire of a cart from Penzance was seven shillings, while John

The Logan Stone: 'a finger's weight can rock it, a man's strength cannot dislodge it.'

Berryman earned three shillings for taking a message to St Just. I'm sure, however, that the expense Lieutenant Goldsmith most resented was in respect of '60 men of St Just who did nothing but drink beer to the value of 13/6'.

An old print in the Logan Rock Inn shows graphically the difficulties involved in the restoration: gigantic wooden beams festooned with pulleys and dozens of sweating men heaving away to replace the fallen stone. All the same it now rocks far less freely than it did before.

THE GIANTS OF TRERYN

The stone must have possessed a peculiar atmosphere of evil for it was also said to be the haunt of a treacherous young giant who ousted his chief and stole both his wife and his castle. Most legends, like fairy-tales contain a strongly moral element and a satisfying measure of poetic justice. Baddies like Tregeagle either die in the gutter, or in the absence of earthly retribution, rot in hell for eternity.

The story of the giants of Treryn, however provides a striking exception to this rule, for the evil-doers not only profited from their treachery but appeared to suffer no ill-effects, either here or in the hereafter. The Iron Age cliff castle, still visible at Treryn Dinas, was conjured from beneath the sea by a giant who lived there and commanded all the lands west of Penzance. He was skilled in the Black Arts and in a holed rock in the cliff, still called Giant's Lock, he put a key in the form of a round stone and prophesied that if it were ever removed, Treryn Castle would disappear under the sea.

The giant was chief of all the West Cornwall giants, but although they swore allegiance to him each year, there was a traitor among them. One handsome young giant lived in a cave in the pile of rocks under the Logan stone. He fell in love with his chieftain's wife and when she encouraged his advances, the two planned to usurp the Treryn giant and reign in his place. One day, while the giantess was sitting on the rock which is still called the Giant Lady's Chair and her husband was snoring lightly on his rock — called, surprisingly enough the Giant's Chair, and likewise still visible — the wicked lover tiptoed up behind his chieftain, as quietly as any giant can, and stabbed him in the belly with a long knife. The Treryn Giant fell

over the cliff to the level ridge below, mortally wounded, but even then he was not allowed to die in peace for his rival leapt down and kicked him into the sea to speed his end. The guilty pair then took over Treryn Castle and, confounding the moralists, lived happily ever after.

ST LEVAN

A mile or so from Treryn is the village of St Levan, home and namesake of the patron saint of anglers. Like St Neot, St Levan existed on a diet of one fresh fish each day, which he caught himself. He used to rest after the day's fishing on a rock on the south side of his church near Land's End. As an old man, close to death, he struck the rock a mighty blow with his fist, splitting it open as it still is today. He then prayed over it and spoke a prophecy:

> *When with panniers astride,*
> *A pack-horse one can ride*
> *Through St Levan's stone,*
> *This world will be done.*

The width of the fissure has not increased noticeably for centuries, so despite warnings of doom and destruction, the world looks good for a few years yet.

On another occasion, when St Levan was out fishing, he caught two bream on one hook, but as he needed only one, he tried to throw the other back. Miraculously, both fish insisted on being caught, so Levan kept them and on his arrival home, found his sister, Breage, waiting for him with two hungry waifs. St Levan cooked the fish and the story ends on a note of inexplicable menace, for the children began to eat ravenously but neglected to remove the bones and choked to death, perhaps as retribution for their imperfect table manners. Until recently, bream were known as 'choke-children' around Land's End.

Despite his piety, St Levan did not suffer fools gladly and refused to fast on the Sabbath, considering his monotonous diet penance

◀St Levan Church.

enough. As he set out one Sunday on his daily fishing expedition, a local woman named Joanna who was gathering herbs and vegetables for her meatless dinner, stopped him, as self-righteous as today's vegetarians, to complain that he was breaking the Sabbath. St Levan argued that gardening was as bad as fishing, but she continued to protest so strongly that the Saint became incensed and calling her a fool, swore that any babies born in the parish and christened Joanna would grow up equally stupid. Since then, no St Levan babies have been christened Joanna, but a piece of ground near the church is still known as Joanna's Garden.

THE TRAGEDY OF SWEET WILLIAM AND FAIR NANCY

Close to St Levan, on the cliffs at Hella Point is a patch of land known as Nancy's Garden. Here a tragic love story was enacted from which Porthgwarra received its nickname, Sweetheart's Cove. Nancy, the daughter of a rich farmer, loved William, a sailor who had once been one of her father's serving men. The farmer considered William unworthy of his daughter and forbade him to visit the house, so instead the lovers stole out at night and met in secret, vowing everlasting fidelity, Nancy swearing that she would never marry another man, William replying that dead or alive, he would one day claim her as his bride.

Their vows were soon tested severely, for William went back to sea and no news came of him until everyone except Nancy was convinced that he had forgotten her. True to her promise, she refused to meet a soul, but mooned about the farm gazing despairingly out to sea from a place on the cliffs at Hella Point which was later called Nancy's Garden. Gradually the grief turned her wits and she went quite mad, refusing to eat or speak, but rocking herself to and fro, looking out to sea for the ship that never came. One night she thought she heard William tapping at the window and calling to her as if from a great distance, to come to him: 'Sleepest thou sweetheart? Awake and come hither my love. My boat awaits us at the cove. Thou must come this night or never

◄Churchyard of St Levan, the patron saint of anglers.

be my bride.'

Transformed with joy, Nancy dressed and hurried to the cove and was never seen again. The same night, William appeared to his father, telling him that he had come for his bride and bidding him farewell. Next day came the news that half way across the world, William had been drowned at sea.

THE PIRATE OF TREGASEAL

Tragedies at sea are a recurring theme in many of the most powerful tales, though in the case of shipwrecks, one man's tragedy is another man's livelihood. Many Cornishmen looked on wrecks as rightfully theirs, but few, even in the depths of famine would deliberately lure ships onto the rocks themselves, preferring to profit from, rather than cause misfortunes, a case of

Thou must not kill but needs not strive
Officiously to keep alive.

This laissez-faire attitude was shown very clearly in 1619 when John Killigrew of Arwenack built a lighthouse on the Lizard, and the locals complained that he was 'taking away God's Grace from them'. 'Meaning,' wrote Killigrew, 'that they now shall receive no more benefit from shipwrecks.'

One man who had a much more positive approach to wrecking was a pirate so wicked that his own crew had thrown him overboard off Tregaseal, near Land's End, where he settled and began to terrorise the countryside. He made his living by luring ships on to the rocks with a lantern tied round the neck of his horse which he led up and down the shore after dark. Passing vessels took this to be the stern light of a ship and assumed that they would find plenty of sea-room around it. Both the ships and their crews were treated savagely, and even if shipwrecked sailors managed to reach land, the pirate showed them no mercy, staving in their skulls with a hatchet and cutting off their hands as they tried to grasp the ledges of the rock.

◄Sweet William and Fair Nancy: 'Thou must come
this night or never be my bride.'

During his life, the old wretch brought countless scores of ships onto the rocks, but he eventually suffered a fate which amply repaid him for his murderous life.

As he lay on his deathbed, around harvest time, two men mowing barley in a field near his house felt an intense calm, as if the world were holding its breath. Suddenly a breeze ruffled the barley and a great voice breathed:

'The hour is come but the man isn't come.'

Looking out to sea, the men saw a black, heavy, square-rigged ship with all her sails set, moving in smoothly against both wind and tide. There was no sign of her crew and she seemed to sail in a pool of darkness. The sky above her became as black as night and she came on unchecked until the tops of her masts were close against the cliffs. The storm descended directly onto the cottage where the dying pirate lay, although the rest of the country was bathed in bright sunlight. The men left their work and ran to the cottage where a crowd of frightened neighbours waited outside for the parson to come.

Inside, the wrecker was howling in agony: 'The devil is tearing at me with nails like the claws of a hawk! Put out the sailors with their bloody hands. The flames are licking round me even now.'

The parson and the doctor went into the room with two of the bravest fishermen. They later described how one minute the room was as dark as the grave, the next second lit by an unearthly brilliance so strong that they could see each hair on the old man's head standing on end in his terror and agony. The black cloud from the ship entered the wrecker's house, shaking it with a dull throb and roar, like a colossal piston, then as suddenly as it had come, it passed and rolled back to the ship which glided quickly away amidst flashes of lightning and awesome thunderclaps.

The pirate lay dead, his eyes wide and bulging in horror, his mouth set in a snarl of fear. The villagers quickly coffined his body and carried it to the churchyard, but although he was a tall man, the coffin felt as light as if it were empty. A black pig joined the procession for a short while but vanished again as suddenly as he had come. When the procession reached the churchyard stile, a

Tol Pedn Coastguard's lookout: countering the power of Madgy Figgy?▶

storm like the one brought by the death ship descended upon it and the bearers rushed into the church for safety. From inside they watched the storm raging long and violently and suddenly a blaze of light, brighter even than the lightning, set fire to the coffin which was borne out to sea, blazing and tossing wildly in a whirlwind which had no earthly origin and a distinctly infernal destination.

MADGY FIGGY

Belief in witches and the practice of witchcraft has always been widespread in Cornwall, and although nowadays the local papers delight in sensational headlines of the 'Shock Witchcraft Expose!' variety, today's witches are merely continuing the traditions of centuries.

Madgy Figgy, one of Cornwall's most famous witches who lived near Tol-Pedn in Penwith, is commemorated by the great chair-shaped rock which now bears her name. It is said that she possessed second sight as well as the knowledge of black magic, and when a wreck was imminent, she would sit in her stone chair, gazing out to sea, gloating and rubbing her hands. Once the ship had foundered on the rocks, Madgy would fly down on a stalk of ragwort — a more traditional mount of witches than even a broomstick — and hover above the scene of plunder, always choosing the choicest treasures as her share. As the villagers were frightened of her supernatural powers, they willingly gave her everything she asked for, in return for her protection, and, some say for her help in the very wrecking itself.

On one occasion, an Indiaman was wrecked and the body of a young and beautiful woman was washed ashore, adorned with rich jewels: opals, topazes, rings of sapphires and rubies and loveliest of all, a necklace of lozenge-shaped emeralds, each surrounded by a cluster of tiny diamonds. Madgy Figgy claimed the body for herself, stripping it of all its jewels and burying it at the top of the cliff. On the night of the burial, a strange, blue light settled above the grave then moved onto the witch's chair. The same thing happened each night and Madgy wondered uneasily what it portended. A stranger

Land's End cliffs: 'stacked together . . . like heaped sugar lumps.'▶

from a foreign country appeared in the village and after watching the grave until the light appeared, he followed it into Madgy's hut where it rested upon the chest containing the beautiful lady's jewels. Madgy realised that the stranger's power was greater than hers and sadly gave him each of the priceless trinkets.

'One witch always knows another, dead or living,' she said.

LYONESSE

With all her black arts and her knowledge of past and future, Madgy Figgy would certainly have known the truth of all the mysterious and compelling tales of the land of Lyonesse which later sank beneath the sea. It's the place where Tennyson sets Camelot itself and he describes it powerfully in *The Passing of Arthur*.

> *Then rose the king and moved his host by night,*
> *And ever pushed Sir Modred league by league,*
> *Back to the sunset bound of Lyonesse,*
> *A land of old, upheaven from the abyss*
> *By fire to sink into the abyss again,*
> *Where fragments of forgotten peoples dwelt*
> *And the long mountains ended in a coast*
> *Of ever-shifting sand, and far away,*
> *The phantom circle of a moaning sea.*

Surely the lost country beyond Land's End of which the kite-shaped archipelago of the Isles of Scilly was once the highest mountain range. It is said that Lyonesse was a fine, rich land with 140 churches and busy cities. It was destroyed by a freak tidal wave and the only survivor was a man named Trevilian who galloped to safety at Perranuthnoe on a white horse. The Trevilian arms still show a white horse outpacing the waves, and in their stables, the family ever afterwards kept a similar steed, saddled and ready in case another emergency arose.

For the Cornish fishermen, the land of Lyonesse is very much a

Lyonesse: '. . . easy to imagine the jumble of towers and spires and ringing church bells.' ▶

reality. For hundreds of years they have netted strange tools, pots and bones from the thirty-mile stretch of water between the Scillies and the mainland.

Medieval writers too treated the land as an accepted fact. In 1584 John Norden, the famous map-maker mentioned Lyonesse in his *Description of Cornwall* while Richard Carew in his *Survey of Cornwall* declares in translucent style:

'The encroaching sea hath ravined from it the whole country of Lyonesse, together with divers other parcels of no little circuit, and that such a Lyonesse there was, these proofs are yet remaining. The space between the Land's End and the Isles of Scilly, being about thirty miles, to this day retaineth the name in Cornish "Lethowstow", and carrieth continually an equal depth of forty or sixty fathoms, (a thing not usual in the sea's proper dominion) save that about the midway there lieth a rock which at low water discovereth his head.' (The Seven Stones Reef).

William Borlase, 150 years later, describes in *The Natural History of Cornwall* how on 1 November 1755, an earthquake which killed 300,000 people in Portugal caused the seas off the west coast of Cornwall suddenly to rise by ten feet, and many people suggest that a similar phenomenon could have caused the seas to flood Lyonesse.

On the Isles of Scilly themselves, crumbling stone walls and the foundations of buildings running mysteriously into the sea are still visible at low tide. Some Scillonians refer to the treacherous Seven Stones Reef as 'The Town', perhaps because the town of Lions is thought to have stood near the reef. This is just one of many mysteries.

The number of chambered barrows or burial mounds littering the islands is disproportionate to the number of people who could have lived there, but as megalithic man usually buried his dead on hilltops and as the Scillies would have been the hills of Lyonesse, the combined population of the lost land and the present islands could account for the numbers.

Another theory to explain the number of graves is that the Scillies were once the islands of the dead where ancient man sailed from the mainland bringing his most eminent corpses for burial. It is perhaps this notion which survives in many haunting accounts such as

◀ Dr Syntax's Head: Land's End.

Tennyson's, in which, after the Last Battle, three queens transport Arthur by barge 'dark as a funeral scarf from stem to stern' to 'the island-valley of Avilion,

> *Where falls not hail or rain or snow,*
> *Nor ever wind blows loudly.'*

Whatever the truth about Lyonesse, only the most unimaginative would declare that the accounts are merely necessary myths of an ancestral splendour, invented by the Cornish to compensate for present poverty. Certainly, economic deprivation creates a fertile climate for the growth of belief in a magnificent past, but there are far more powerful reasons for that belief's survival. The tales of Lyonesse convey a deep impression of an inexplicable, and timeless significance, ringing with the religious echoes they share with so many of the Cornish stories. Above all, the tales possess sheer narrative genius, likewise shared by all the County's most lasting legends; genius which over centuries has inspired diverse talents to pass them down by word of mouth and in noble, joyous poetry and prose.

Standing on the great cliffs at Land's End, some dropping sheer to the sea, some stacked together and descending in tiers like heaped sugar lumps, the land of Lyonesse seemed very close to the surface. Close to the surface both of the waves themselves and of the consciousness of all who love Cornwall and Scilly. A slight haze made the middle distance of the seascape bluely indistinct and it was easy to imagine the jumble of towers and spires and ringing church bells which so many people — the stolid as well as the imaginative — claim passionately to have seen and heard.

For me it was a moment of slight sadness mixed with fulfilment: the end of a journey that over several months had taken me from end to end and from coast to coast of Cornwall, leading me into a tapestry garden of legends and stories rivalling the world's greatest myths. Then my mood lifted. I had learned the great lesson that the supply of Cornish legends is rich and literally inexhaustible and that a lifetime would be too short to visit all the sites and hear all the versions. Because of that, this book has scarcely scratched the

◀Land's End cliffscape.

surface and my journey has been only the first stage in an exploration which so far has constantly dazzled and delighted me. I only hope that *Legends of Cornwall* will inspire other people — visitors and Cornish men and women — to follow in my footsteps and experience that splendid thrill of discovery for themselves.

Longships from Land's End: 'The Land of Lyonesse seemed very close to the surface.'▶

BOOKS CONSULTED

Sir John Betjeman, *A Shell Guide, Cornwall*

William Borlase, *The Antiquities of Cornwall* and *The Natural History of Cornwall*

W. Bottrell, *Stories and Folklore of West Cornwall* and *Stories and Traditions of West Penwith*

Richard Carew, *The Survey of Cornwall*

M.A. Courtney, *Cornish Feasts and Folklore*

Tony Deane and Tony Shaw, *The Folklore of Cornwall*

Daphne du Maurier, *Vanishing Cornwall*

Brenda Duxbury, Michael Williams and Colin Wilson, *King Arthur Country in Cornwall, The Search for the Real Arthur*

S.L. Enys, *Cornish Drolls*

F.E. Halliday, *A History of Cornwall*

J. Henry Harris, *Cornish Saints and Sinners*

Robert Hunt, *Cornish Folk-lore* and *Cornish Legends*

John Norden, *Description of Cornwall*

Sir Arthur Quiller-Couch, *Cornwall's Wonderland*

G.W.R., *Legend Land*

C.A.R. Radford and M.J. Swanton, *Arthurian Sites in the West*

Donald Rawe, *Traditional Cornish Stories and Rhymes*

Barbara C. Spooner, *John Tregagle of Trevorder, Man and Ghost*

ALSO AVAILABLE

OCCULT IN THE WEST
by Michael Williams. Over 30 photographs. Price £1.50.
Michael Williams follows his successful *Supernatural in Cornwall* with further interviews and investigations into the Occult — this time incorporating Devon. Ghosts and clairvoyancy, dreams and psychic painting, healing and hypnosis are only some of the facets of a fascinating story.
'. . . *provides the doubters with much food for thought.*'
Jean Kenzie, Tavistock Gazette

SUPERNATURAL IN CORNWALL
by Michael Williams. 24 photographs. Price £1.50.
'. . . *a book of fact, not fiction . . . covers not only apparitions and things that go bump in the night, but also witchcraft, clairvoyancy, spiritual healing, even wart charming . . .*'
Jenny Myerscough on BBC
'*Serious students of ghost-hunting will find a fund of locations.*'
Graham Danton on Westward TV

MY CORNWALL
A personal vision of Cornwall by eleven writers living and working in the county: Daphne du Maurier, Ronald Duncan, James Turner, Angela du Maurier, Jack Clemo, Denys Val Baker, Colin Wilson, C.C. Vyvyan, Arthur Caddick, Michael Williams and Derek Tangye, with reproductions of paintings by Margo Maeckelberghe and photographs by Bryan Russell. Price £1.50.
'*An ambitious collection of chapters.*'
The Times, London

KING ARTHUR COUNTRY in CORNWALL, THE SEARCH for the REAL ARTHUR
by Brenda Duxbury, Michael Williams and Colin Wilson.
Over 50 photographs and 3 maps. Paperback £1.20; hardcover £2.95.
An exciting exploration of the Arthurian sites in Cornwall and Scilly, including the related legends of Tristan and Iseult, with The Search for the Real Arthur by Colin Wilson.
'. . . *provides a refreshing slant on an old story linking it with the present.*'
Caroline Righton. The Packet Newspapers

ALSO BY SALLY JONES
LEGENDS OF DEVON
48 illustrations. Price £1.75.

OTHER TITLES INCLUDE

CORNWALL & SCILLY PECULIAR
by David Mudd £1

FOLLOWING THE TAMAR
by Sarah Foot £1.20

HOME ALONG FALMOUTH & PENRYN
by David Mudd £1.50

TINTAGEL TO BOSCASTLE
by Michael Williams 75p

DEVON MYSTERIES
by Judy Chard £1

PENZANCE TO LAND'S END
by Michael Williams and John Chard 75p

ABOUT ST JUST IN PENWITH
by Frank Ruhrmund 90p

THE LIZARD
by Jill Newton £1.20

DOWN ALONG CAMBORNE & REDRUTH
by David Mudd 95p

THE FALMOUTH PACKETS
by David Mudd 75p

ABOUT THE CITY, A Portrait of Truro
by David Mudd 90p

ABOUT MEVAGISSEY
by Brenda Duxbury 75p